Understanding My Emotions

When I'm Angry

Understanding My Emotions

When I'm Angry
When I'm Embarrassed
When I'm Happy
When I'm Lonely
When I'm Overwhelmed
When I'm Sad
When I'm Scared
When I'm Sorry
When I'm Surprised
When I'm Worried

Understanding My Emotions

When I'm Angry

ALEXANDRA DALTON

**Understanding My Emotions
When I'm Angry**

Copyright © 2016 by Village Earth Press, a division of Harding House Publishing. All rights reserved. No part of this publication may be reproduced or transmitted in any form or by any means, electronic or mechanical, including photocopying, recording, taping, or any information storage and retrieval system, without permission from the publisher.

Village Earth Press
Vestal, New York 13850
www.villageearthpress.com

First Printing
9 8 7 6 5 4 3 2 1

Series ISBN (paperback): 978-1-62524-440-6
ISBN (paperback): 978-1-62524-376-8
ebook ISBN: 978-1-62524-132-0
    Library of Congress Control Number: 2014944102

Author: Dalton, Alexandra.

Contents

To the Teacher	7
When I'm Angry	8
Find Out More	42
Feeling Words	44
Index	46
Picture Credits	47
About the Author	48

To the Teacher

More than a hundred years ago, John Dewey insisted that the true purpose of schooling was not simply to teach children a trade but to train them in deeper habits of mind. Social-emotional learning builds on Dewey's theory further, suggesting that emotional skills are crucial to both academic performance and future success in life.

The research is definitive: emotional training is good for children! A recent study, reported in the *New York Times*, found that preschoolers who had even a single year of social-emotional training continued to perform better two years after they left the program; they were less aggressive and less anxious than children who hadn't participated in the program. Another study found that K-12 students who received some form of emotional instruction scored an average of 11 percentile points higher on standardized achievement tests. A similar study found a nearly 20 percent decrease in students' violent behaviors.

The goal of this series of books, UNDERSTANDING MY EMOTIONS, is to instill in young children a foundation of emotional intelligence. Use these books to help your students learn to understand, identify, and regulate their emotions. Give them important tools that will serve them well for the rest of their lives!

When I'm Angry

Sometimes I just feel mad!

It's how I feel when something isn't fair.

Like the time when I thought I was going to spend a week with my grandmother. I was all packed and everything. And then my mom said I couldn't go after all. My mom said she needed me to stay home instead. I was angry!

I was so angry that I yelled and screamed and stomped my feet. I told my mom I hated her. I said lots of mean things to her.

The next day, though, I was sorry I'd said all those things to my mother. I was sorry I'd gotten so mad.

My mom said she understood why I was mad. My mom said I didn't need to be sorry for getting angry. It's just a feeling inside me. She said everybody gets angry sometimes. She gets angry at my dad. But being angry doesn't last forever. People get over being mad. And when they do, they need to say they're sorry if they did something mean while they were angry.

Being angry is just one of the feelings I have inside me. I have lots of other feelings too.

When my mom told me I could go see my grandma next week instead, I felt happy.

I felt scared the time I saw a giant spider crawling up the wall!

I felt surprised and startled the time I looked out the window and saw a black bear in our backyard. I wasn't expecting to see THAT!

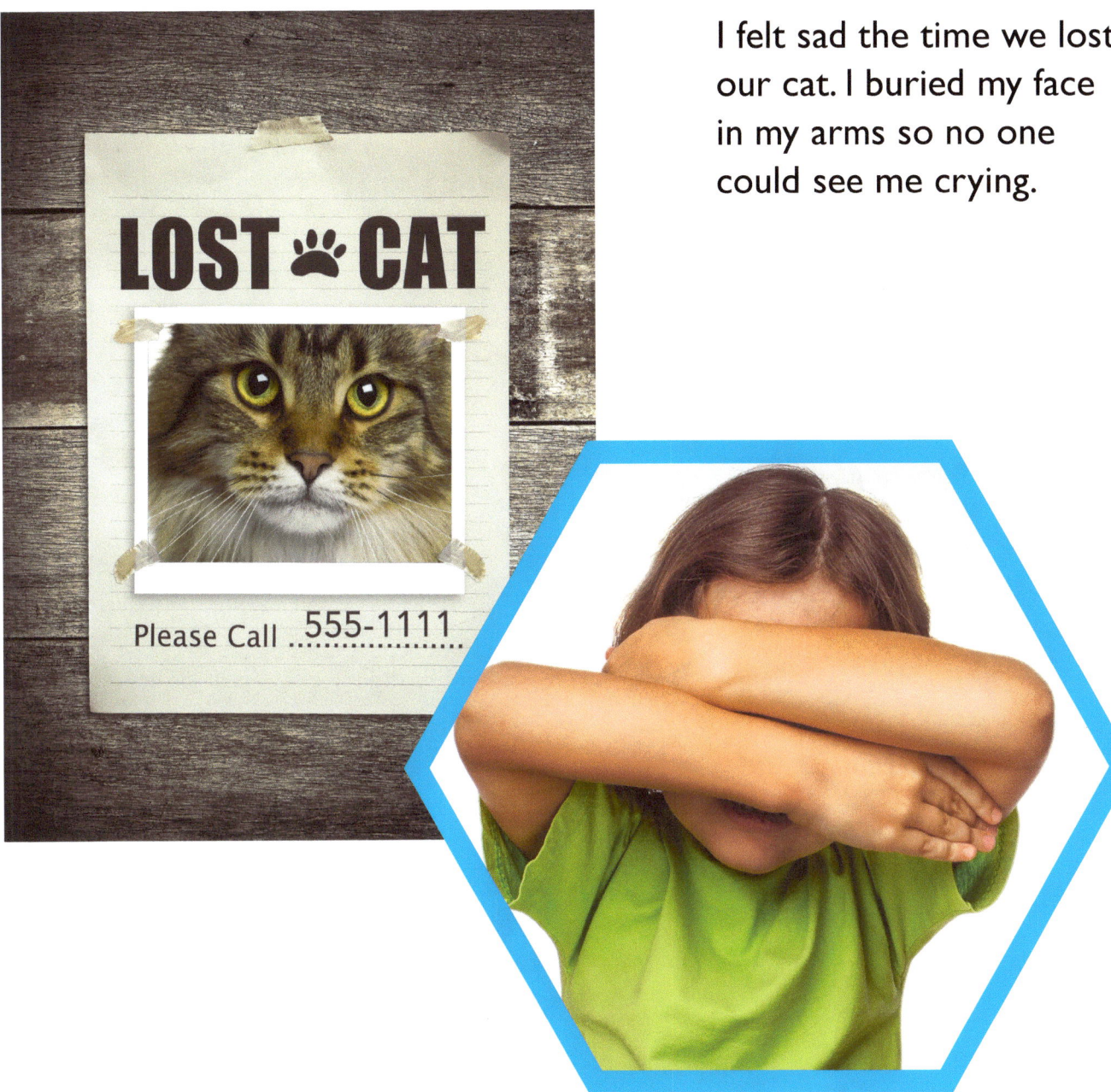

I felt sad the time we lost our cat. I buried my face in my arms so no one could see me crying.

When my cat came home, I was very, very, VERY happy!

When I don't understand something at school,
I feel confused and puzzled.

All these feelings—sad and happy, surprised and puzzled, scared and angry—are just some of the feelings I have. These feelings are called emotions. Emotions show up on our faces. People can tell what we're feeling by our mouths and our eyes.

I have lots of different emotions. Everyone does. These feelings are coming and going inside us all the time.

Things that happen around us make us happy or sad, angry or scared—but the feeling happen INSIDE. Emotions take place inside our heads.

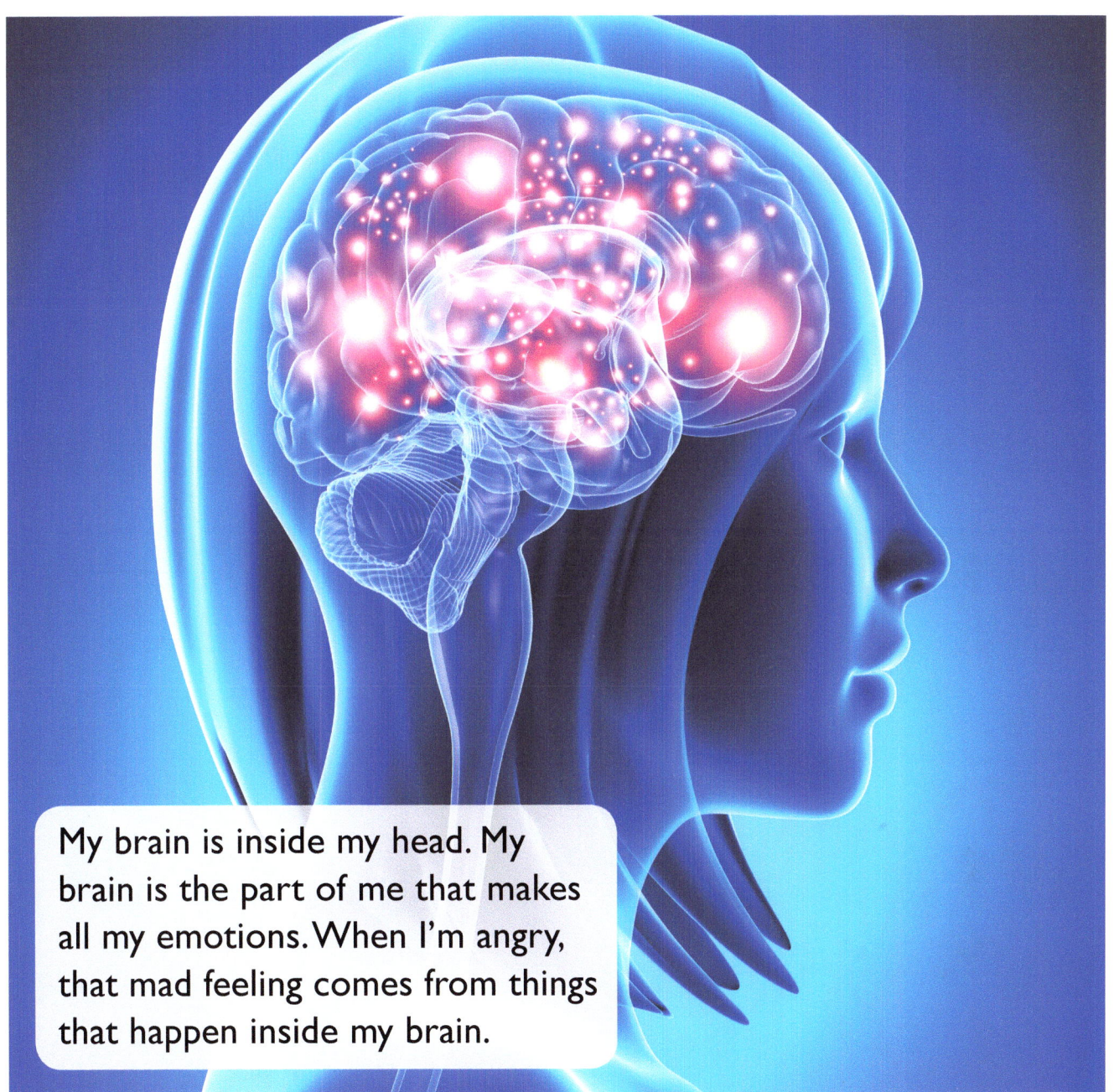

My brain is inside my head. My brain is the part of me that makes all my emotions. When I'm angry, that mad feeling comes from things that happen inside my brain.

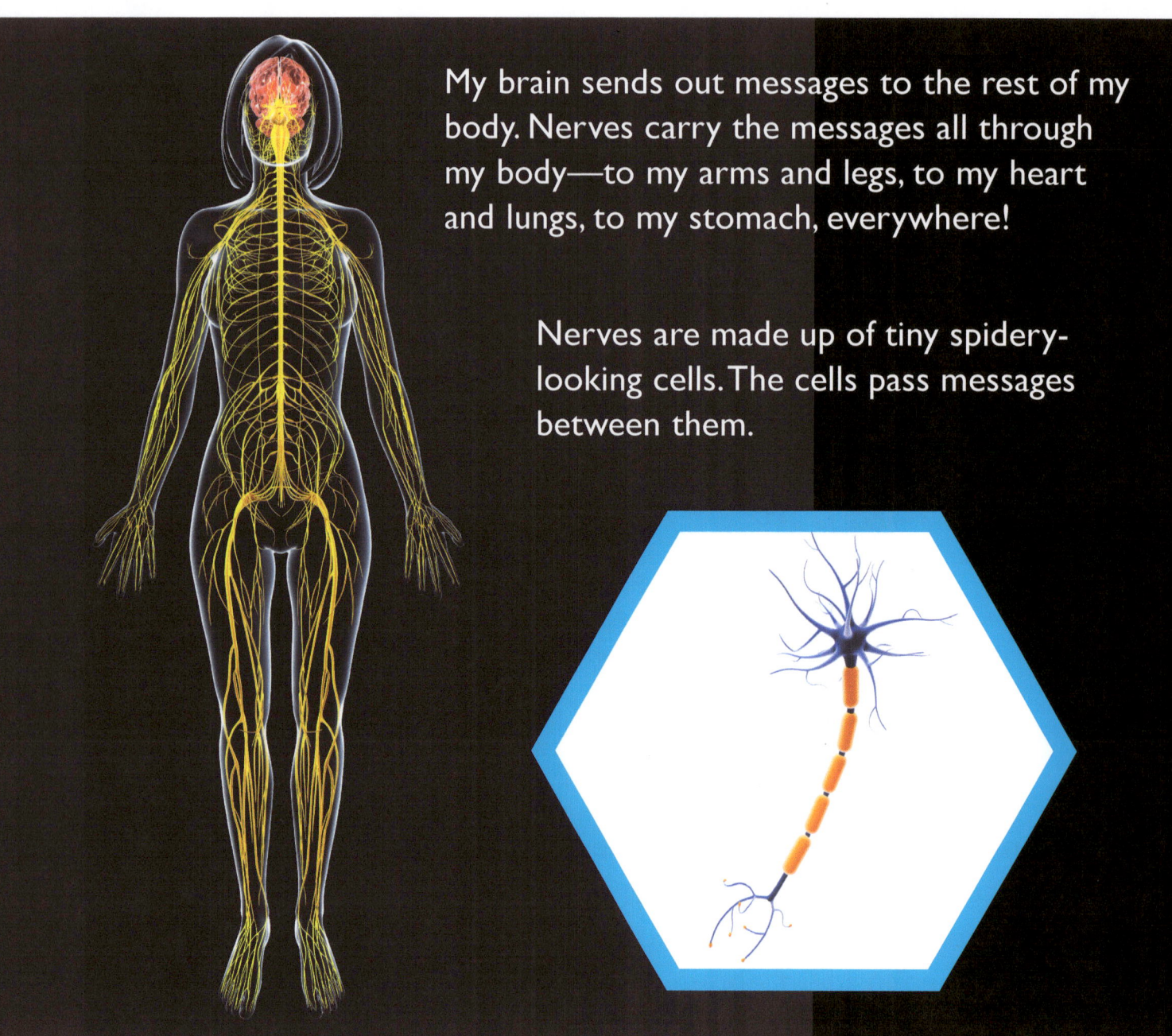

My brain sends out messages to the rest of my body. Nerves carry the messages all through my body—to my arms and legs, to my heart and lungs, to my stomach, everywhere!

Nerves are made up of tiny spidery-looking cells. The cells pass messages between them.

These messages make the rest of my body do things too when I'm angry. My heart beats harder. My face feels hot because my heart is pushing more blood through my body—and some of it is going to my face. That's what makes my face look red.

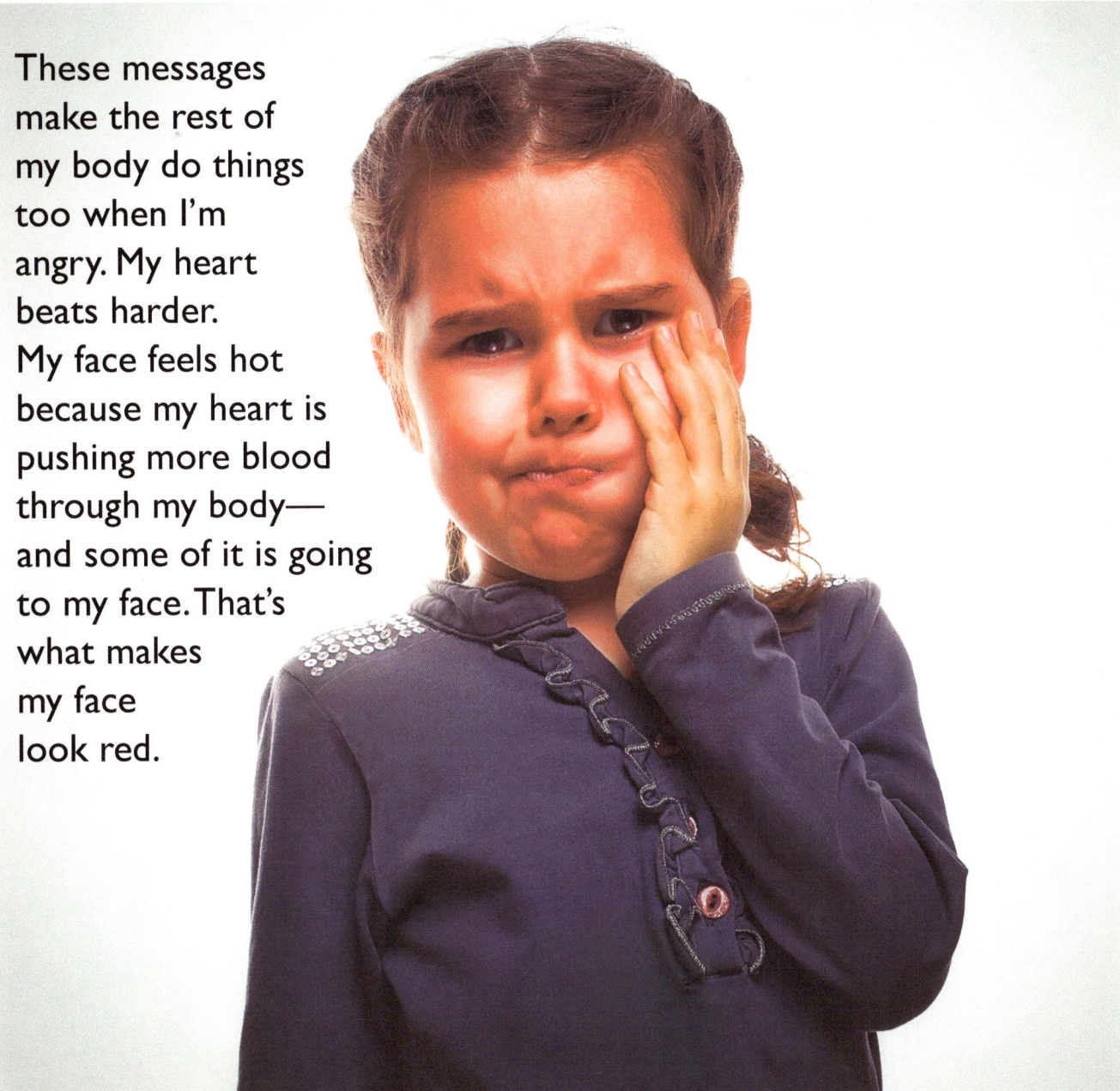

Different things make me angry. I feel frustrated when I can't do something I want to do—like ride my new bicycle. Feeling frustrated can turn into mad feelings.

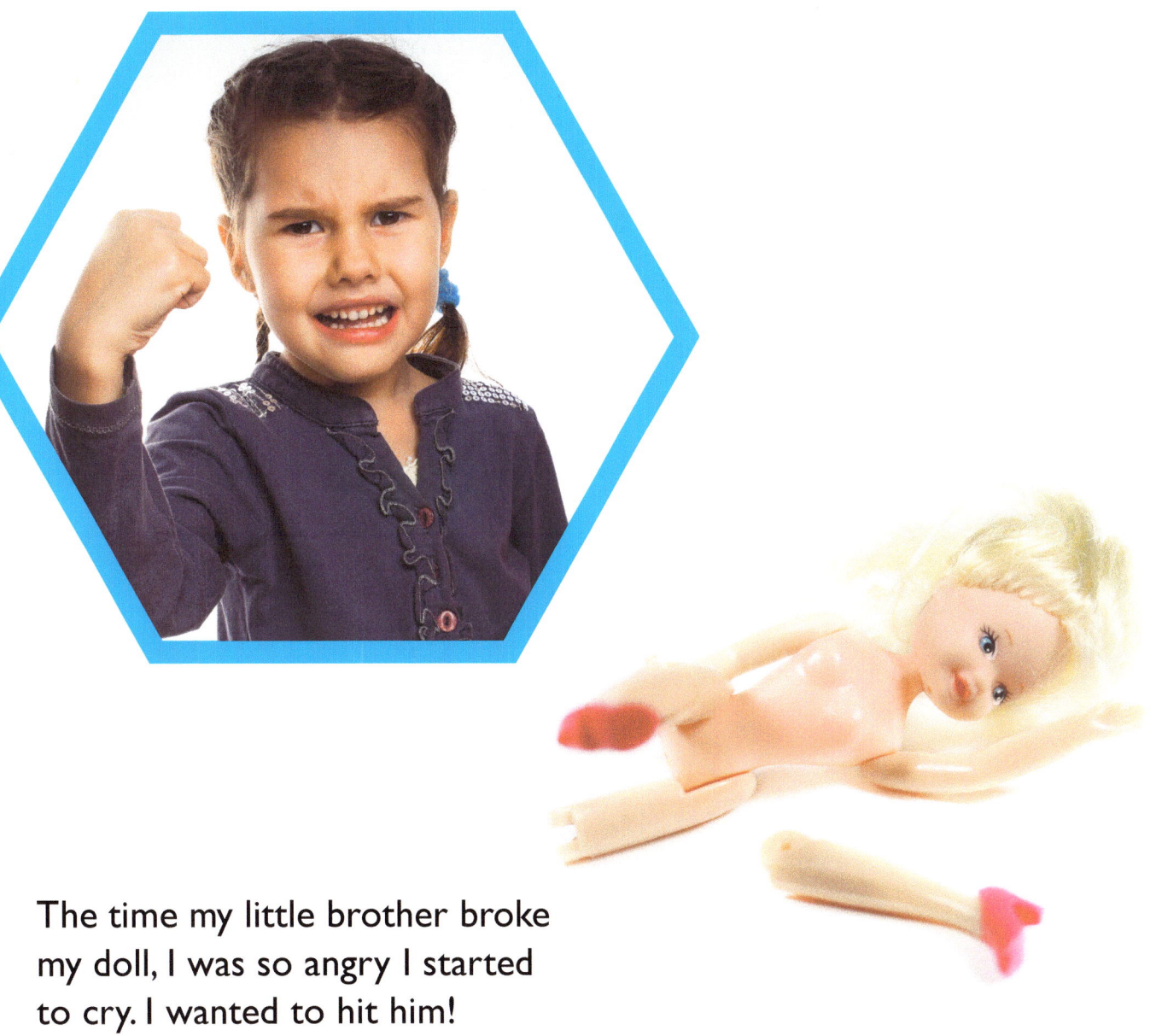

The time my little brother broke my doll, I was so angry I started to cry. I wanted to hit him!

My mom says it's okay to feel angry—but it's never okay to hurt someone! No matter how mad I am, it's not okay to make my little brother cry.

It's never okay to hit or kick. It's not okay to throw things or break things when I'm angry.

My dad says there are things I can do when I get angry that will help me handle the mad feelings. Then I won't let my mad feelings hurt people.

One of the first things I need to do is know when I'm mad. I need to know that my brain is sending out angry feelings. The feelings are inside me. They belong to me—not to the outside world. So when I'm mad at my brother, he's not a bad little boy. When I'm mad at my mother, she's not a bad mom. When I'm mad at my bike because I can't ride it, it's not my bike's fault! All those feelings are inside my head. I can give them a name. I can learn to get control of them.

When I know I'm angry, I can give myself time to calm down. I can go for a walk. Or I can sit in a quiet place by myself for a while.

When I'm by myself, it's okay to yell and scream a little. It won't hurt anyone if I do.

But once I calm down a little, I can think about what happened. I can try to see the other person's point of view. I can understand that it wasn't my mom's fault that I couldn't go to my grandma's when I wanted to go. And my little brother didn't mean to break my doll!

Grownups aren't so different from kids. My dad says that when my mom screams at him, he doesn't want to listen. But once she listens to his side and starts to understand how he feels, their angry feelings go away.

Another way to deal with angry feelings is to look for solutions. A solution is an answer—or a way to fix a problem. So when my mom said I couldn't go visit my grandma, we talked about it. We tried to think of another time when I could visit her.

When I was frustrated I couldn't ride my bike, I asked my dad to help me.

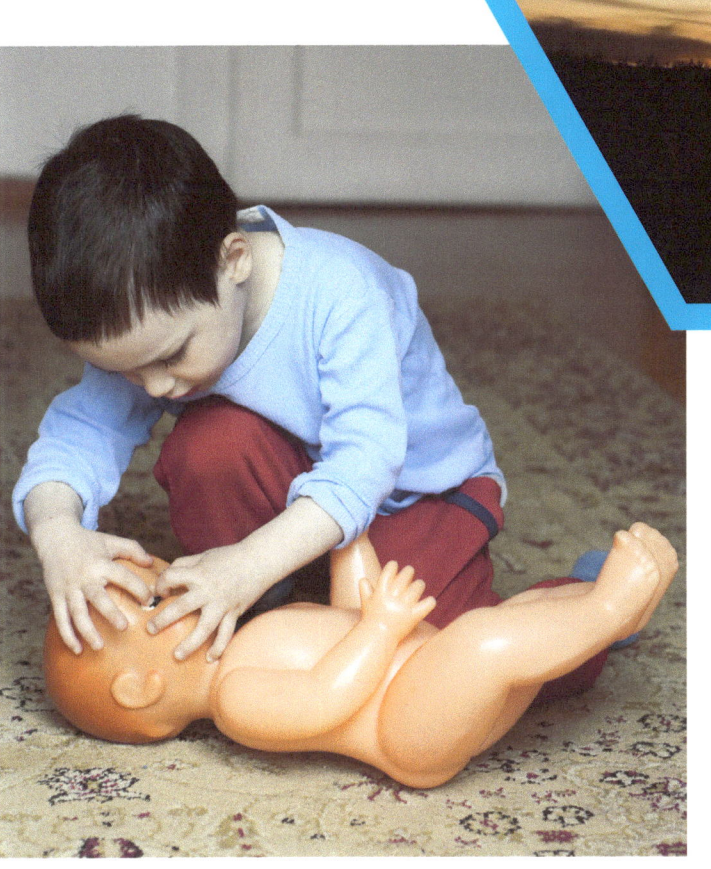

I gave my little brother his own doll to play with, so he wouldn't want to play with mine.

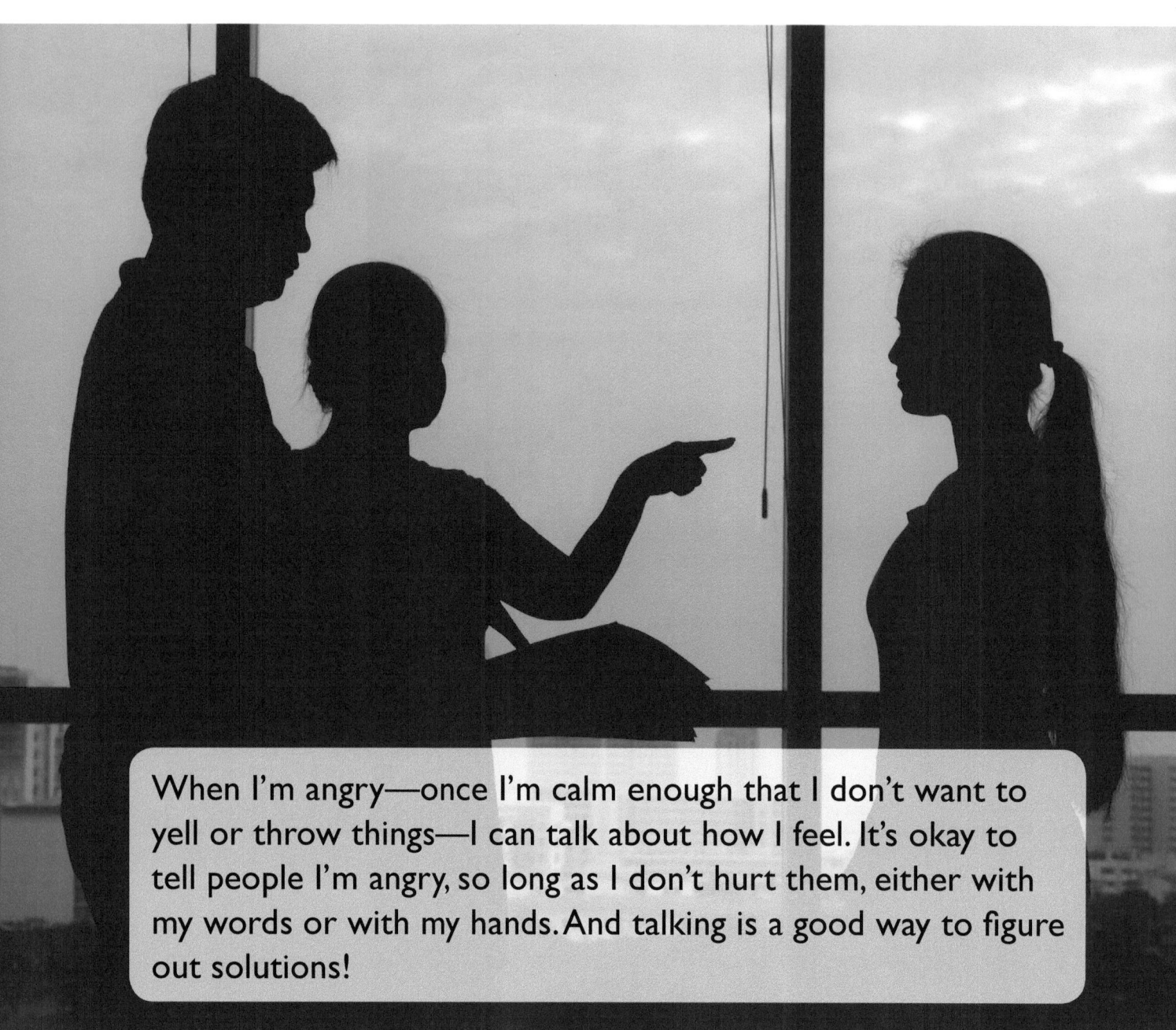

When I'm angry—once I'm calm enough that I don't want to yell or throw things—I can talk about how I feel. It's okay to tell people I'm angry, so long as I don't hurt them, either with my words or with my hands. And talking is a good way to figure out solutions!

But sometimes everyone gets mad and says and does things they shouldn't. When I do that, I need to apologize. I need to say I'm sorry! It's not always easy to say I'm sorry—but if I hurt someone, I need to make it right.

Everyone gets mad sometimes. It's just one of the feelings we all have. Now that you know that, here's what comes next—learn to handle your mad feelings. Here are some things you can do:

- Give your feelings a name. Those mad feelings are called ANGER. When you know you are feeling angry, that will help you not to blame other people. Your feelings belong to you—and only you can learn to control them!

- Find a place to be alone. When you're alone, you won't do something that might hurt someone. You can take time to think.

- Try to see the other person's point of view. They probably didn't mean to make you mad—and if they did, they had a reason!

- Look for solutions. Is there something you can do to help fix things?

- Talk about your feelings. It's okay to let people know you're angry, so long as you don't let your mad feelings hurt others.

- If you've hurt someone, say you're sorry! Ask them to forgive you for doing something mean.

And remember—everyone gets mad sometimes!

Find Out More

You can learn more about your emotions by going online and checking out these websites. Some of the sites have videos you can watch or games you can play. You could also read the other books in this series to find out more about feelings—or you could go to your library and see if you can find the books listed on the next page. There's a lot more you can learn about worry and other feelings!

On the Internet

It's My Life: Emotions
pbskids.org/itsmylife/emotions

KidsHealth: Feelings
kidshealth.org/kid/feeling

Model Me: Faces and Emotions
www.modelmekids.com/emotions_dvd.html

In Books

Aliki. *Feelings*. New York: Greenwillow Books, 2007.

Huebner, Dawn. *What to Do When Your Temper Flares: A Kid's Guide to Overcoming Problems With Anger*. Washington, DC: Magination Press, 2007.

Krueger, David. *What Is a Feeling?* Seattle, WA: Parenting Press, 2013.

Meiners, Cheri. *Cool Down and Work Through Anger*. Minneapolis, MN: Free Spirit, 2010.

Mulcahy, William. *Zach Gets Frustrated*. Minneapolis, MN: Free Spirit, 2012.

Rotner, Shelley. *Lots of Feelings*. Minneapolis, MN: Millbrook Press, 2003.

Snow, Todd. *Feelings to Share from A to Z*. Lake Elmo, MN: Maren Green, 2007.

Feeling Words

Angry is just one of the words we use when we talk about feelings. But there are many more words that describe feelings. Here are some of those words.

Excited

Scared

Embarrassed

Worried

Guilty

Hurt

Proud

Lonely

Shy

Sorry

Surprised

Bored

Index

An index is a way you can quickly find something inside a book. The numbers tell you exactly what page to go to if you want to find that word.

apologize 39

blood 25
brain 23–24, 31
brother 27–28, 31, 34, 37

calm down 32, 34
confused 19
crying 17

emotion 20–23, 42
eyes 20

face 17, 20, 25, 42
feeling 13–14, 20–23, 26, 30–31, 35–36, 40–44, 48

frustrated 26, 37, 43

grandma 14, 34, 36
grownup 35

happy 14, 18, 20, 22
head 22–23, 31
heart 24–25
hurt 28, 30, 33, 38–39, 41, 44

mean 11, 13, 34, 41
mother 12, 31
mom 10–11, 13–14, 28, 31, 34–36
mouth 20

nerves 24

problem 36, 43
puzzled 19–20

sad 17, 20, 22
scared 15, 20, 22, 44
solutions 36, 38, 41
sorry 12–13, 39, 41, 45
startled 16
surprised 16, 20, 45

talk 38, 41, 44
think 34, 36, 41

Picture Credits

p. 9 © Maxximmm | Dreamstime.com
p. 10 © Maxximmm | Dreamstime.com
p. 11 © Maxximmm | Dreamstime.com
p. 12 © Maxximmm | Dreamstime.com, © Cowardlion | Dreamstime.com
p. 13 © Alexandre Miguel Da Silva Nunes | Dreamstime.com
p. 14 © Maxximmm | Dreamstime.com
p. 15 © Maxximmm | Dreamstime.com, © Melinda Fawver | Dreamstime.com, ©
p. 16 © Maxximmm | Dreamstime.com, © Rgbe | Dreamstime.com
p. 17 © Maxximmm | Dreamstime.com, © Isselee | Dreamstime.com, © Win Nondakowit | Dreamstime.com
p. 18 © Maxximmm | Dreamstime.com, © Isselee | Dreamstime.com
p. 19 © Maxximmm | Dreamstime.com, © Oneblink | Dreamstime.com
pp. 20–21 © Bettie Watts | Dreamstime.com
p. 22 © Alain Lacroix | Dreamstime.com
p. 23 © Shubhangi Kene | Dreamstime.com
p. 24 © Shubhangi Kene | Dreamstime.com, © Milan Martaus | Dreamstime.com
p. 25 © Maxximmm | Dreamstime.com
p. 26 © Susan Leggett | Dreamstime.com
p. 27 © Elena Loginova | Dreamstime.com, © Maxximmm | Dreamstime.com
p. 28 © Tuthelins | Dreamstime.com
p. 29 © Povarov | Dreamstime.com
p. 30 © Alexandre Miguel Da Silva Nunes | Dreamstime.com
p. 31 © Maxximmm | Dreamstime.com
p. 32 © Eugenesergeev | Dreamstime.com
p. 33 © Maxximmm | Dreamstime.com
p. 34 © Maxximmm | Dreamstime.com
p. 35 © Alexandre Miguel Da Silva Nunes | Dreamstime.com
p. 36 © Maxximmm | Dreamstime.com
p. 37 © Yobro10 | Dreamstime.com, © Pavla Zakova | Dreamstime.com
p. 38 © DragonImages | Dreamstime.com
p. 39 © Maxximmm | Dreamstime.com
p. 40 © Maxximmm | Dreamstime.com
p. 44-45 Fotolia: © Fasphotographic, © Cantor Pannato, © Andres Rodriguez, © Gabriel Blaj, © Moodboard Premium, © Halfpoint, © Cantor Pannato, © Blend Images, © Zhekos, © Olly, © Wavebreak Media Micro, © Muro

About the Author

Alexandra Dalton was a teacher, and now she is a writer. When she was a teacher, she helped her students talk about their feelings. She knows that it's hard work sometimes to talk about our feelings—but she knows we feel better and we get along with each other better when we can use our words to talk about how we feel. Alexandra has three children. She also has a dog and a cat and four goats. She lives in New York State.